Plants in Differen

by Barbara Mitchell

Contents

Longman

Edinburgh Gate
Harlow, Essex

Seaside Plants

Seaside plants have a hard life. There is no soil – only sand to grow in. There are strong, salty winds, too. Some seaside plants can protect themselves from the wind. Others have long roots that reach down to find water.

Some plants help to form sand dunes. One of these is the marram grass. You will find lots of it at the seaside. It has long roots that grow deep into the sand. They stop the salty winds from blowing the plant away. The roots also hold the sand together, making a ridge. This ridge is called a dune.

Marram grass

When the tall grasses are growing well, smaller plants grow between them. Sea rocket likes to grow between grasses. It has creeping stems. The sand can build up around them.

Sea bindweed grows along the beach, too. This plant binds itself to the sand. It cannot get blown away. It spreads quickly – just like the bindweed that grows in gardens.

marram grass

sea rocket

sea bindweed

Seaside plants can protect themselves in different ways. The yellow horned poppy has hairy leaves. The hairs hold drops of water. These keep the plant damp and healthy.

In dry weather, the marram grass rolls its leaves into thin tubes. These thin tubes trap the damp air. This keeps the grass alive.

The sea holly has thick, waxy leaves. They stop the plant from getting too dry. It has prickles on its leaves – like holly.

Further back from the sea, there is more shelter from the wind. Shorter grasses can grow more easily and cover the dunes. Heather may grow there, too. It flowers in autumn. Some flowers are pink or purple, some are white. Some people think that heather is lucky.

Pond Plants

Lots of people have ponds in their gardens. The ponds can be full of plants growing in the water. Some float on top of the pond. Some grow under the water so you can hardly see them.

Some plants grow in deep water. Their roots are in the mud. These plants have thin stems. They don't need thick stems because the water holds them up. Their flowers stick up out of the water.

meadowsweet

water iris (yellow)

duckweed

Some plants float on top of the pond. Duckweed is like this. Its roots hang free in the water. Duckweed grows very quickly. If you don't take some out, it can cover the pond.

Water lilies have big flat leaves that float on the water. They have beautiful flowers, too. The flowers can be white or yellow or pink. People plant water lilies in plastic baskets. The baskets sit on the bottom of the pond. The roots grow out into the mud.

water iris
(blue)

reeds

water
forget-me-not

water lily

Lots of different plants grow by the edge of the pond. Here the water is shallow.

Plants that grow in shallow water are often tall. They have strong underground roots. They help to hold the plants up. Water irises are like this. They also have thick stems. They flower in the spring. Their flowers can be white or yellow or purple.

9

Reeds grow by the edge of ponds, too. A long time ago, people used to cut the reeds. They used them to make thatched roofs for houses. You can still see some of these roofs today.

Plants that like soft damp soil grow on the bank of the pond. Many of them have brightly coloured flowers. The water forget-me-not has blue flowers. The meadowsweet has white ones.

water forget-me-not    **meadowsweet**

All pond plants are different. Some like to live in deep water. Some like to live in shallow water. Some like to live on the bank. They each have their own special place.

11

City Plants

Cities can be very dirty places. Cars and buses give off exhaust fumes. Many trees cannot grow because of the pollution, but there are some which can. In London, plane trees grow in the streets – they don't mind the traffic at all.

There is a strip of land down the middle of some wide roads. This is called the central reserve. Trees and bushes are often planted there. Bush roses grow well in spite of the pollution. In summer they have lots of flowers. In autumn they have red hips which hungry birds like to eat.

Plants make cities look prettier. All the people who are living in the city, working there or visiting can enjoy them.

In the middle of cities, there is often a park. Most of them have been there for many years. The trees have grown very tall and they help to block out the noise of traffic.

People go to sit in the parks – they like to get away from the noise and the traffic. They like to look at the wonderful displays of flowers. The city gardeners often plant bright geraniums and busy lizzies and pansies. These plants will flower all through the summer.

Some people live in city flats. They don't have gardens, but they often grow plants in window boxes. If they have a balcony they can grow bigger plants in tubs. The plants must be watered every day, because the soil in the pots and window boxes can soon dry out. The plants will die if they are not watered.

City houses often have gardens. There might be old brick walls round some of them. Roses and clematis like to grow up walls to reach the sun. Ivy will grow in shady parts.

If there is enough space, people plant vegetables. They grow carrots or runner beans or cabbages, which they pick and eat for dinner. People say that their home-grown vegetables taste delicious!

Plants in Hedgerows

Long, long ago, farmers planted hawthorn hedges around their fields. Hawthorn bushes grew thick and prickly. So they made good hedges to keep animals in the fields. When the hawthorns grew too tall, the farmer cut the tops off.

You can still see hawthorn hedges in the country. In May, it has pretty white blossom.

As the hedges grew, seeds from other plants fell onto the soil. Trees and shrubs like ash, elm and willow began to grow with the hawthorn. Holly grew in hedges, too. Its leaves are thick and prickly. In winter the holly has red berries, which birds love to eat.

brambles

holly

You can often see climbers in hedgerows. One is called honeysuckle. This has pretty flowers with a wonderful smell. The Romans brought honeysuckle to Britain hundreds of years ago.

Brambles grow in hedges, too. They have long prickly stems. In the autumn, they have small round fruits called blackberries. You can pick them and take them home to eat – but wash them first!

honeysuckle

snowdrop

violet

primrose

Many flowers grow in the hedgerow. In winter, snowdrops push through the snow. They are one of the first flowers of the year. Primroses and violets soon follow.

cow parsley   **foxglove**   **hogweed**

Later in the year, you can see taller plants. They have odd names such as cow parsley, hogweed and foxglove. The foxglove has mauve flowers. Parts of the foxglove can be used as a medicine. But this plant is poisonous, too – so take care!

Some hedges are very old. This is how you find out if a hedge is old or not. Look at hedges near to where you live. Count the different trees and shrubs in 30 meters of the hedge. If there are lots of them, the hedge is very old. If there is only one sort of shrub, the hedge is not so old.

Plants in Woods

Woods are made up of trees and other, smaller plants. Trees that grow in colder parts of the country are often evergreen. This means that they do not lose their leaves all at once in autumn.

A pine forest in Scotland

Trees such as pines can survive long, cold winters because their leaves are like needles. They don't dry out in the bitter winter winds.

All year round, evergreen trees block out the light from the forest floor. Most plants need light to make food and to grow. But the sun can only reach the ground where there is a gap in the trees. Some grasses will grow in these spots. Low plants such as bilberries and wild strawberries can grow, too.

bilberry

wild strawberry

In the warmer parts of the country, different trees grow in woods. Trees such as the oak, ash, beech and birch grow well.

oak

ash

birch

beech

They have broad leaves that cast a heavy shadow on the ground. These trees are called deciduous. In the autumn they lose their leaves, and they are dormant or resting all through winter. Then, when the weather gets warmer in the spring, new leaves begin to grow.

In early spring, deciduous trees have no leaves to make shadows, so the sun can reach the forest floor and the ground becomes warmer. Plants begin to grow in the sunlight. Beautiful flowers bloom, such as wood anemones, primroses and bluebells.

primrose   **bluebell**   **wood anemone**

Fungi are different from other plants. They need
moisture but they do not need sunlight. They cannot
make their own food. They live by feeding on other
plants. Many fungi live on dead plants and animals.
Many live on fallen leaves, rotting wood or the trunks
of trees. A dark, damp forest is a perfect place for
fungi to grow. But watch out – some are poisonous!

Plants in Fields

Plants have been used for food for millions of years. We eat different parts of plants. Sometimes we eat the fruit, sometimes we eat the roots and sometimes we eat the stems and the leaves. Farmers grow the plants for our food in fields.

fruit

roots

leaves

Some farmers grow wheat. During the summer, wild flowers often grow in the wheat fields. Tall, white daisies and red poppies look beautiful in the golden wheat.

In autumn, farmers harvest the wheat. The most important part is the ear at the top of each stem. These are ground into flour and made into bread. Farmers also use the stalk of the wheat, which is called straw. Farm animals sleep on it in winter.

Sometimes we eat the roots of plants, such as carrots, parsnips or potatoes.

If you plant a potato, it will send green shoots above the ground. The roots will grow deep under the ground. They will swell into lots of small new potatoes, which you can dig up and eat. If you leave them in the soil, they will grow bigger. Soon, they will be big enough to dig up and make chips!

new potatoes   **old potatoes**

Sometimes we eat the leaves of plants. The cabbage is one of these. They are planted in long rows.

Weeds often grow among the plants and choke them. Diseases might attack the plants, too. The farmers use machines to spray crops with chemicals. This might kill the weeds and the disease but it can also kill wild flowers, insects and birds.

Some people think there is a better way to grow the plants that we eat. This is to choose plants that can survive disease and difficult weather conditions. These plants can be grown without using chemicals. This method of growing food is called organic farming. More and more people who grow fruit and vegetables in their gardens are using this method.

Index of Plant Names